**W9-CPF-776**

# SEE STOK RUN

## STOCKS MADE SIMPLE

GRAY PURDY

*inkVoice*
PUBLISHING

*inkVoice*
**PUBLISHING**
PO Box 9049, Seattle, WA 98109 USA

Printed in the USA
First Edition

Purdy, Gray.
    See stok run : stocks made simple / by Gray Purdy.
    p. cm.
    Includes bibliographical references.
    LCCN 2007922760
    ISBN-13: 978-0-9792209-1-3
    ISBN-10: 0-9792209-1-2

    1. Stocks.  2. Investments.  3. Finance, Personal.
    I. Title.  II. Title: Stocks made simple.

HG4661.P87 2007                    332.63'22
                                   QBI07-600065

# CONTENTS

## FAIR WARNING & FAIR WISHES

The stock market is a wild unpredictable place; invest at your own risk! Neither the publisher nor the author bear any responsibility for your investment decisions or results.

Whatever path you take with your investments, we join in wishing you an enjoyable journey through life, with the hope that you may find a way to live peacefully and respectfully with all forms of life on this bright blue planet we share.

To my parents,
who taught me to laugh at myself,
and my mistakes,
of which there are many.

# 1

# Simplicity

Ideas won't keep;
something must be done about them.

*- Alfred North Whitehead*

Do we build complicated castles in the sky when attempting to invest in stocks?  Must we painstakingly struggle to understand a complex labyrinth of details, or are the answers so simple we could draw them in the sand with a stick?

Some professionals work very hard at investing and achieve ordinary results, while many amateurs generally ignore their stocks, and do very well.  Strange but true.  Why?

If you are reluctant to invest in the stock market, you need not be.  If you are already invested but not paying attention to your portfolio, it doesn't have to be a boring or confusing endeavor.  If you read your brokerage statements, but find them unenlightening, there is a more intuitive path.

### It's not hard, it just looks that way!

Investing with See Stok Run™ is about being able to quickly see what's important.  It is a guide to clearing away the fog and unnecessary complexities of the market.  Forget having to think your way through a series of details just to understand your own portfolio!  Through the use of probability theory and simple imagery, easy yet powerful risk management methods are revealed.  Profitable investing is simply not that hard.

This book is about managing stocks in a way that fits with your risk comfort level, as well as your ethical concerns.  It is written for those who have a long term view of their investment objectives and are willing to guide their path to profit in a disciplined way without wasting time.

## Book & Software

See Stok Run is the title of this book as well as the name of animated software developed to bring visual clarity to the stock market.  I started investing in stocks when I was still a kid, and have reduced a lifetime of investment observations into the few simple concepts presented here and within the software seestokrun.com.  It was my thinking about stocks that lead to the creation of the software in the first place, so the book and the software complete a circle of thought regarding an intuitive visual style of portfolio management.

## What Not Tool

See Stok Run is investment neutral.  It can be used in conjunction with all sorts of investment methods.  It is simply a conceptual and visual tool.

This is **not** a method for short term, or "get rich quick" people, day traders, or those who can't afford to risk some of their capital in the stock market.

## Live Stock & Stok

I grew up on a cattle ranch where the word stock referred to animals.  Ranchers are direct people, who say what they think and don't fancy things up.  There is no letter 'c' in Stok because it's not needed.  It doesn't really do anything, so I took it out. This is a main point of the See Stok Run philosophy; take the fancy bits out and get to the point. My objective is to strip away what's not helpful, and clarify what is.

## PERSONAL FINANCE

If you are just starting to enter the stock market, make sure you find out how the trading or brokerage system you will be using works before investing. The harsh reality is that the stock market was not created for your benefit! The stock market was created to gain access to people's money (like yours), and it does this very effectively. If you do benefit, it is a side effect the market makers couldn't care less about. If you are impatient or unrealistic, there are plenty of experts who will sing the song you want to hear and harvest your wealth.

In terms of personal finance, I offer only these two basic guidelines:

- Never borrow money to invest in the stock market. Stocks are uncertain and unknown, while debt is certain and known. One is a chance, the other an obligation; they are not similar.

- Never invest more than your can risk, and never invest more than half your net worth in stocks.

## MORE INFORMATION

The End Notes and Glossary contain words and additional useful information not mentioned elsewhere in the book.

*"Are you sure my stock just went down in sympathy?"*

# 2

# STANDARDS

> Money won't buy happiness,
> but it will pay the salaries of a
> large research staff to study the problem.
>
> *- Bill Vaughan*

There are scores of investment methods, yet there is no solid evidence which points us to the perfect one. They all produce different results at different times.

Typically people deal with their stocks one of three ways:

1. They **delegate** the task to someone else.

2. They use the theory of **fundamental** value.

3. They use the theory of **technical** pattern recognition.

**Delegation** places your money at the mercy of someone else. This could be good or bad depending on who they are, what is motivating them, and their skill level.

**Fundamental** value investing considers the factors that create value within a company. The assumption is the value of a company will eventually cause its stock price to rise proportionately. This is the most widely accepted theory and has the appeal of being tied to the finances and growth potential of the companies stocks are based on. This approach requires research and experience to accomplish well. Besides the reported attributes of a company[1], other critical information determining a company's fate might rest with a competitor, a commodity, the labor market, or within the geopolitical realm.

**Technical** trading is based on price and volume movement pattern recognition. The assumption is that stock price movements will repeat recognizable patterns. This is the favorite method of day traders, since patterns can play out in mere minutes. It can be complex and require large amounts of time and skill, or be accomplished by computer.

## NON-PROFESSIONALS

If you don't want to become a full time professional investor, it seems like you must choose between delegation, or struggling to follow one of the two common time consuming methods. I say "it seems like," since this book will defy that conclusion, and present simple yet powerful ways you can use to manage your own stock market investments without spending much time at it.

## REDUCTION

See Stok Run extracts powerful elements of portfolio management and reduces their complexity to easily understandable elements. To do this, we will borrow from both the fundamental and the technical realms, add in some probability theory to create a cohesive logic, and then complete the picture with visual tools to make it easy.

## THEORIES

Market theories are guesses at cause and effect relationships that may or may not exist. Is it going up because of the fundamentals, or the technical pattern, or because of what the Fed just did? Who knows? Rather than promoting a theory about why things might happen, or should happen, the focus is on what **is** happening and what can be done about it.

## THE BEST WAY

The book See Stok Run is mainly a bunch of ideas, a range of options, which are designed to expose key influences of portfolio management. See Stok Run software provides tools that bring these factors alive and makes them obvious. Use whatever method of investing you like; this is not about persuading you to invest as I do, or even to use the ideas presented if they don't seem smart to you.

As far as I can tell, if someone did invent the very best way to invest in the market on some magic day, it would become less so quickly. Things are constantly changing. Actions beget reactions. People are continually figuring out new ways to gain however and whenever possible. What is best this year, will likely not be the next.

See Stok Run provides a menu of suggestions, not a recipe you must or even should follow. If I succeed in raising your awareness or confidence as an investor, then I have succeeded. But determining the best way for you to trade is up to you.

## EMOTIONS

No matter how smart we are, the thing that can derail all logic, is emotion. Attempt to develop the cool mind of a mathematician when dealing with stocks, or they will drive you nuts.

# 3

# BASICS

A child of five would understand this.
Send someone to fetch a child of five.

*- Groucho Marx*

Although the stock market is a convoluted environment, in the final analysis, it all comes down to doing two things:

**BUY**

**SELL**

These two actions will determine how well you fair with any stock. No matter what you're thinking, whether you have the most sophisticated supercomputers, or a rotary dial telephone; these two actions alone will determine the outcome.

It is interesting that once you buy a stock, your reasons for buying it instantly become irrelevant. If one person has a Ph.D., and another a grade school education, and they both buy a 100 shares of a stock, they will both experience the same exact results. The shares of stock don't care what we think or know, and the price of the stock will not be effected by our cleverness or lack thereof. Research, technical or fundamental, is only worthwhile if it convinces you to buy or sell. Only the simple acts of buying and selling will create the results.

## TAKING CHANCES

Investing in the stock market is about taking chances, and therefore it is useful to consider probability theory as a part of the process. Probability theory demonstrates that nothing is for certain, and sometimes we may lose. If we are on the right side of probability, the more chances we will have, and the better the odds are we will prevail. What are the factors that determine how many chances you get?

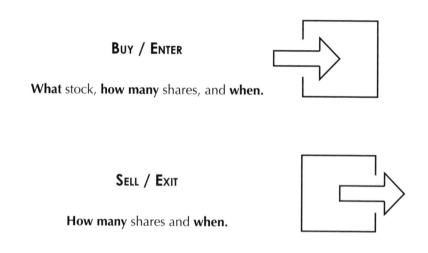

### BUY / ENTER

What stock, how many shares, and when.

### SELL / EXIT

How many shares and when.

As we look at what you can do to influence your investments, we will examine each one of these elements, all of which are at your command.

## ENTER - SELECTION:  WHAT STOCK TO BUY?

Selecting which stocks to buy is the decision that gets all the attention. Picking the right stocks can certainly boost your value. There are several views on how to do this.

### ENTER - NUMBER:  HOW MANY SHARES TO BUY?

The number of shares you buy of each stock will determine your risk exposure in that stock.  You can easily adjust these numbers to fit your desired risk levels.

### ENTER - TIME:  WHEN TO BUY?

Entering the market at different times will produce different results.  You can become aware of the overall market influences to your advantage according to your style of investing.

### EXIT - NUMBER:  HOW MUCH TO SELL?

Knowing how many shares to sell is a subject often completely overlooked.  Mathematical solutions can add clarity and power to your portfolio.

### EXIT - TIME:  WHEN TO SELL?

Knowing when to exit, either to control losses or capture profits, is a critical decision that many investors ignore to their peril.

4

# Dᴀʀᴛꜱ

A dog that walks around
will find a stick.

*- Japanese proverb*

Around 1988, someone at the Wall Street Journal got the idea of testing the effectiveness of random stock selection. Each month they threw darts at stock names to pick them for hypothetical purchase. Then, these pretend portfolios were placed in competition with the selections of professional stock analysts. Six months later the performance results were compared. These contests continued for many years and were published in the Wall Street Journal under the story heading: The Darts vs. The Pros.

Logic suggests that the application of well ordered knowledge would have a strong advantage, but amazingly that was not the case. On many occasions over a period of years, the random wanderings of darts outperformed some of the most well informed, experienced investment minds.

ORDERED

— — —

— — —

— — —

That the professionals won sometimes is not surprising. The fact that the darts frequently won is disturbing if you believe brain power should be able to do better than a random selection. If we average all these years, the professionals do come out slightly ahead, but only by a small margin. Now consider how you, a non-professional, might do in competition with those same darts.

If we let go of the idea that we can know what will happen in the future, we can see that the darts succeed because they express probability and chance in the ever unpredictable market. They stumble into unknowable advantages.

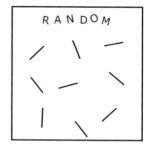

Our world is being redefined more rapidly than ever. No matter how much you study, you can only base your opinion on what is known today, and that will change as soon as tonight.

MAYBE THE LESSONS THE DARTS TEACH ARE:
- NO ONE KNOWS WHAT WILL HAPPEN NEXT, SO WHY PRETEND?
- ANYONE CAN PROFIT, IF THEY TAKE ENOUGH CHANCES.

## MONKEY BUSINESS

There is even a monkey[2] who picks stocks! So far he's beaten all the major indexes four years in a row. Does he know what he's doing, or are probability and chance at work?

# 5

# CASINO

> Success is simply a matter of luck.
> Ask any failure.
>
> *- Earl Wilson*

A casino boss operates quite differently than a gambler. Casino managers don't waste their time thinking in terms of luck, they focus on mathematical probability. For them it is not gambling but logic. They are playing with numerical advantage on their side such that they are extremely likely to profit. They don't care if one person wins, because they know most gamblers are losing. They know this because they have painstakingly run the mathematical odds on every variation of every game against the number of players and the amounts of their bets.

If we only play one hand of cards, we will not get a good picture of how probability influences the game. However, if we play fifty times, we will be able to see percentage results emerge. Since the casino boss is effectively playing thousands of hands an hour, she can precisely quantify the probable outcome.

THIS CASINO STYLE OF THINKING CAN BE
APPLIED TO PORTFOLIO MANAGEMENT.

In a casino each game starts when the cards are dealt or the wheel spins. Usually 100% of your bet is at stake, and the game ends quickly, regardless of results.

Unlike a casino, and possibly to your advantage, in the stock market you determine the start of the game and you determine the end.  You determine how much risk you will take, in what amounts and at what times.  The "house" in the stock market is the brokerage firm, and they take only a small bit of money for making a trade, instead of all your money if you lose a bet.

As long as you know some basic concepts
and watch what you're doing,
it's pretty simple to
control risk to a great extent.

# 6

# CRASHES

Cheer up! The worst is yet to come!
*- Philander Chase Johnson*

When stocks fall, they usually fall in slow motion;  not always, but usually.  Even during the big market crashes of the past, despite alarming
one day drops, the major percentage declines took months or years to
play out.  The word crash suggests the damage is done in one day, or
even one week, but the facts are quite different from that perception.

### CRASH DECLINE TIME

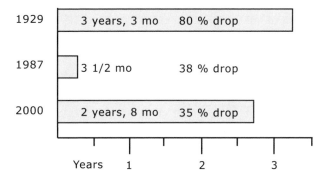

| 1929 | 3 years, 3 mo    80 % drop |
| 1987 | 3 1/2 mo    38 % drop |
| 2000 | 2 years, 8 mo    35 % drop |

Years    1        2        3

People who lose great amounts usually do so by shifting into the denial
mode during a prolonged decline.  Typically they begin with no exit
plan in place.  Then, once a decline is clearly underway they wake up
to the fact that it would have been smart to sell some time ago, but since
they did not, they freeze.  Day after day they watch their stocks drop,

refusing to acknowledge what is happening. Many attempt to console themselves by saying things like "It'll bounce back," or "I've lost too much already to get out."

Not wanting to admit even one failure, people tend to hold onto negative positions, while at the same time rushing to sell positive positions before they can realize full growth potential. In this way, emotions lead many to cling to failure and snatch mediocrity from the jaws of excellence.

# 7

# RECOVERY

> `That's the reason they're called lessons.` the Gryphon
> remarked: `because they lessen from day to day.`
> *- Lewis Carroll*

Although we can't know a predictive number on the up side, we can know and quantify the mathematics of recovering from a declined position. As a position drops, the amount of gain needed to recover accelerates.

If we lose 10%, we must gain 11% to recover.

If we lose 30%, we must gain 43% to recover.

If we lose 50%, we must gain 100% to recover.

If we lose 60%, we must gain 150% to recover.

## DECLINE & PROFIT

If our goal is to make a profit, the mathematics of decline become even more dramatic. For example, let's say we start with a dollar and think making a 15% gain (15 cents) in the market is a reasonable goal.

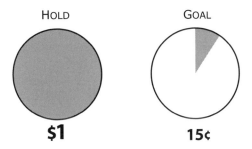

HOLD        GOAL

$1        15¢

If we let that dollar decline by 50%, we are left with only 50 cents.

In order to recover, that 50 cents must double in value. Percentage-wise that requires a 100% gain.

But then, in order to reach our original goal, we need to add in the additional gain required, or 15 cents. Therefore our new goal is to win back the lost 50 cents, plus 15 cents profit, for a total of 65 cents.

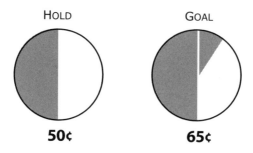

Since 65 cents is 130% of the 50 cents we hold, we now must hope for a 130% profit instead of a 15% profit.

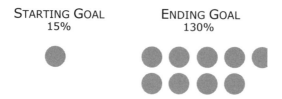

This new goal is 8.6 times that of our starting goal, or 760% more difficult to obtain!

Probability theory applied to the mathematics of decline and recovery has lead me to this conclusion:

PLAN TO LIMIT YOUR LOSSES IN THE FIRST PLACE.
THERE ARE PLENTY OF STOCKS THAT
ARE GOING UP IN AN UP MARKET.

## DOING THE MATH

If you're concerned about having to actually do math to invest well, relax, computers can handle it for you.

*"Count them again. There <u>can't</u> be more trouble spots than there are countries."*

# Risk

> Behold the turtle.
> He makes progress only
> when he sticks his neck out.
> *-James B. Conant*

Wanting to invest in the market without risk is sort of like wanting to go swimming and not get wet. Everything worthwhile in life involves risk. The key is not risk avoidance, but risk management. On the upside, the more you define and control risk, the more likely you will feel comfortable taking risks.

## For Average Results

If you don't want the risk of investing in individual stocks, and will be happy with average returns, then you may want to try index investing. With no work at all you will be likely to beat many, if not most professional investment managers and funds[3]. If you want to avoid the risk of stocks altogether, there are investments which actually have guarantees (like insured bonds).

## Indexes

An index is nothing more than a bunch of stocks that someone decided to track. That's it! No big deal. They pick some stocks, add up the numbers, and presto, you have an average number they call an index. The Dow Jones Industrial Average[4] consists of thirty of the largest companies someone at Dow Jones decided to group together. The S&P 500[5] is comprized of 500 big company stocks chosen by Standard & Poors.

The important thing to understand is that an index represents the average performance of certain stocks while no one makes any investment decisions at all! Indexes are non-managed. The performance of an index is just an expression of what happened, like yesterday's weather report.

### PREDICTABILITY SECURITY PARADOX

In answer to the quest for security, people frequently gravitate toward investing in big companies seeking more predictable results with lower risk. But what is the true goal? If we want financial security, should we seek predictable results, or above average profits? It is true that historically, larger companies tend to behave more predictably than smaller companies, but it is also true that smaller younger companies frequently outperform larger older companies in the stock market.

The interesting thing is that when it comes to stock selection, unpredictability can work to your advantage. Almost every stock that becomes a stellar growth company starts out being relatively unknown and therefore unpredictable. The real finds, are just that, they need to be found. If you find them before they go ballistic, you stand to make much more profit than those who buy them after they advance and become well known.

This situation leads us to the predictability security paradox. People who want to be financially secure, often equate financial security with predictability, but strangely, buying less predictable stocks often yields higher results, leading to greater profits, more capital, and therefore more true financial security.

For those who are cringing right now, remember the wonderful thing about money is that it is easily divided. You could try a certain way of investing with just a small portion of your investable cash, thereby giving an idea a chance that is equal to your risk tolerance for that concept.

# RISK TYPES

There are one hundred men
seeking security to one able man
who is willing to risk his fortune.

*- J. Paul Getty*

Almost all market discussions about risk are centered around future performance. This is the concept of **perceived risk.**

On the other hand, **functional risk** is your practical dollar exposure on
any given day. If I am sitting at my computer, investing in well known
stocks, and the market is open and trading normally, my functional risk
is very low. It is low because I can trade out of any position at any
time.

## PERCEIVED RISK VS. FUNCTIONAL RISK

It is important to know the difference between functional risk and perceived risk when entering the market. For example, if everyone tells you
a company is really risky (perception), but you like it, you think it will
grow (alternate perception), what does the risk warning mean? If it is
trading normally, as long as you pay attention on a regular basis, for you,
the functional risk could be very low. Since everyone's functional risk is
a unique combination of their holdings, trading methods and attention,
everyone's overall risk levels are different. Regardless of perceptions, it
is the functional risk that you will actually experience.

## FUNCTIONAL RISK COMPONENTS

Functional risk in the stock market is measured by three elements:

1. Trading stability
2. Ability to act
3. Capital exposure

**Trading stability** is an attempt to describe price movement and trading volume. Stocks that are infrequently traded or have wildly fluctuating prices, are unstable and volatile.

However, if we look at companies that have profitable businesses and are worth substantial amounts of money -- in other words, most recognizable stocks -- these are relatively stable and our functional risk can be very low. The possibility that a stable stock will drop significantly before someone watching it can react is unlikely.

**Ability to act** includes knowing about a stock's trading price, and the ability to execute a trade based on that knowledge. If we don't know how to place a trade, or we only monitor our holdings once a month, our knowledge is low and our functional risk is high. If we know what we're doing and check our holdings on a regular basis, our functional risk decreases.

**Capital exposure** means how much we have invested in each position. If we have all our money in one stock, we have high functional risk, no matter what stock it is, since our fate depends upon only one stock's performance.

## MONITORING

How much monitoring is required to achieve a good functional risk level? A strategy must fit a practice. If you have a year to year approach, one trading day is a small, rarely important period of time, while an hour is insignificant.

It only takes me one or two minutes a day to check the status of my portfolios using the See Stok Run program. The maximum number of times I check during a day is twice; usually once during the morning and once near or after the market close. Anything more than this is of no use, or is counter-productive to a long term investment vision.

# 10

# Mix

Nothing is so irrevocably missed as
the opportunity which crops up daily.
- *Maria von Ebner-Eschenbach*

Diversification is just a fancy name for a mix or an assortment.  It is an important tool because holding different stocks creates a mixture of results and provides a mathematically significant number of chances.

## Two Flavors

The word diversification is commonly used to describe two situations; one is not really diversification, but a good impostor.

## Averaging

Averaging masquerades as diversification.  This clever mimic looks like diversification, sounds like diversification, but it isn't.  Averaging is when a single investment is invested in many other investments.

For example, a mutual fund may be invested in three hundred stocks and therefore be referred to as a fully diversified fund.  While the fund itself is diversified, its results will be the average of all its holdings, plus the cost of management; in other words, a single result.

Suppose a fund is badly managed, charges excessive management fees, or has an embezzler in house; if something goes wrong, it won't matter that the fund is diversified. You will still lose because you invested in only one company.

Holding an averaged investment can be a useful, but it is not the same as being diversified.

## DIVERSIFICATION

The main point of diversification is to divide your worth into separate and different investments so that if one or more fail, you are likely to have others that survive. There are three components, which together create diversification. They are:

1. The **number** of investments.

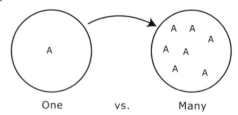

2. The **types** of investments.

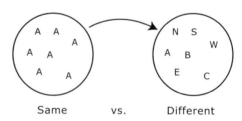

3. The **control** possible.

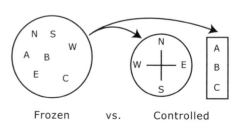

## NUMBER

In order to be diversified you must be invested in several things. On the low end, the mathematics of diversification start to work with just two, and increase dramatically with three. On the high end, once at least ten investments are held, the significance of each additional investment is not so great, mainly due to the second factor, the type of investment.

If you hold just one stock, in a given time period there are only two basic outcomes possible; it will go up or down. The probability of a negative outcome is 50%. However, if you hold two stocks, now there are four possible outcomes and the possibility of a completely negative result drops to one chance in four, or 25%. This represents a dramatic reduction in risk exposure. If we add a third stock to this equation, the chance of a completely negative result drops to just 11%; another significantly large reduction.

As you can see, the mathematical advantage of diversification kicks in right away. With minimal diversity, risk exposure is significantly reduced.

## DIVERSIFICATION EFFECT

| Number of Positions | Possible Results | | | |
|:---:|:---|:---|:---|:---|
| 1 | ● | | ○ | |
| 2 | ●● | ●○ | ○● | ○○ |
| 3 | ●●● ●●○ ●○○ ○○○<br>○●● ●○● ○●○ ○○● | | | |

● = Gain     ○ = Loss

## TYPE

The second component of diversification is the type of investment. If you hold two investments that are virtually the same, they are likely to produce very similar results and therefore partially defeat the mathematical advantage of holding two instead of one investment. In order for diversification to really work, you need to hold investments which are different from each other in at least one significant way.

On a primary level this means investing in different asset classes, sometimes called asset allocation. The four most common asset classes are: stocks, bonds, cash and real estate. If you have a net worth great enough to be invested in all four, you can gain basic overall investment diversification.

To gain a geo-political advantage, you may also want to consider investment diversification among countries as well.

Within the stock market, there are several different industrial classifications of stock. For example, a coal company is considered an energy stock, whereas a children's clothing maker is an apparel stock. The difference between these two types of business is great, so they will likely produce different results at different points in time, which is the whole idea.

If we look at two closely related companies, like children's clothing manufacturing and children's clothing retailing, we are likely to see a sympathetic relationship between the performance of the two businesses. Investing in linked business has the effect of losing some, but not all, potential risk management gain when compared to being diversified among businesses which are dramatically different.

It's easy to diversify between different types of stock because the profiles of companies list the industries they participate in.

## CONTROL

The third component of diversification, control, is often overlooked either because it is assumed or ignored. Control over several investments is the real key to unlocking the power of diversification and discovering staying power in the market.

By control I mean the ability to buy and sell at will, according to performance results and market events. If you lack the ability to react to situations as they are happening, then you're really just along for the ride. If I hold three investments and I learn that one is in trouble, but I can't sell it, then my results will be governed only by a decision made in the past (the decision to buy that holding). However if I have the power to change, I can remove a failing position and replace it with a new chance of success; a chance that is at least unknown, instead of a known failing one.

Most individual stocks are easy to trade, but as soon as we get into other types of investments, many are easy to buy but difficult to sell quickly.

If you find yourself in the unlucky spot of having several of your investments plunging in value, you may find it handy to pull the rip cord and get the heck out. The worst thing that can happen to you by stepping aside is to miss an opportunity to make money. But a missed opportunity is far different than lost dollars. Everyday new opportunities present themselves. However, if you lose your capital, the game is over.

## THE 10% BUY IN RULE

The 10% buy in rule says: Don't purchase a position that is worth more than 10% of your total portfolio value (including investable cash).

This discipline encourages diversification and decreases risk exposure. If you are following this rule, even if the worst possible thing happens to one of your stocks (i.e. it goes bankrupt), you will still have only lost at most 10% of your starting portfolio value. Coupled with the rule of never investing more than 50% of your net worth in stocks, this means you will have lost no more than 5% of your capital value.

## Safety vs. Risk

If your goal is to create an extremely diversified portfolio (of say, more than 30 holdings) you will be heading in the direction of safety. This is great, however the more stocks you hold the more likely your portfolio will become average. One pathway to stellar performance is to hold fewer stocks that perform better than average; however this tips the balance in favor of risk. If you pay attention, that additional risk can be worthwhile. It all depends on your attitude, your management and your comfort level in taking risk.

To illustrate, suppose you invest evenly in 30 different stocks. You will be nicely diversified. But then suppose a wonderful thing happens, and one of the stocks you hold doubles in value, what will this mean? With a portfolio of 30, it will create a portfolio gain of only 3%. With a portfolio of 10, that same stock advance would create a gain of 10%.

Therefore, with diversification, it is a sliding scale. More holdings create more average performance, while fewer holdings create more responsive performance. Responsiveness could be positive or negative depending on which stocks you hold and how you manage them.

# 11

# FLUX

Change is constant.

*- Benjamin Disraeli*

The prices of stocks constantly fluctuate. They meander, taking two steps forward and one back. The larger the price fluctuations, the more volatile the stock, and vice versa.

Price fluctuation can be expressed as a dollar or percentage amount the price of a stock changed in a certain amount of time.

A maximum daily price fluctuation range is the maximum percentage amount a stock price moves in one day over a period of days. For example, if, during 20 days, the maximum price fluctuation in any **one** of those days was 5%, then its daily maximum fluctuation range for that time period would be 5%. This is true even if it only moved a fraction every other day. This is **not** a measure of performance, only an indicator of volatility.

A young highly volatile stock will have a big fluctuation range, while a steady older company will have a small range.

When holding a stock, it's a good idea to know its normal price fluctuation. This is important so that you can identify when unusual price movement occurs. Most financial guides don't report stock price fluctuations as such.

The See Stok Run software program provides a simple display of maximum fluctuation ranges over the 20, 50 and 200 day time periods. This provides a good representation how much meandering a stock tends to do. Without such a display, you can still make a guess by studying historical graphs.

## PRICE GAP

To make things more interesting, not only do stock prices fluctuate during trading hours, they change in after hours trading sessions, and they change overnight. When the price of a stock opens higher or lower than it closed the previous session, the difference is called a price gap. SeeStokRun.com takes this into account by calculating fluctuations inclusive of after hours changes or gaps.

## BETA

Beta is another way to look at a stock's price volatility. The Beta of a stock is an expression of how one stock's volatility compares to the rest of the market. It is a multiplication factor. So a Beta of 1, means a stock is normal. A Beta of 2, means that as the market average moves, that stock price will tend to change twice as much. A Beta of 0.5 would express a stock that has half the normal volatility, and is therefore twice as stable as the market.

## VOLATILITY VS. PERFORMANCE

Volatility could be good or bad depending. More volatile stocks can drop more quickly, but they can also rise more quickly. Your choice will depend on your risk tolerance.

# 12

# VOLUME

Enough! no more:
'tis not so sweet now as it was before.

*- Edward de Vere, 17th Earl of Oxford*

No matter what selection method you use, checking a stock's average trading volume is smart. This is especially so with small companies.

The average trading volume of a stock is simply how many shares of the stock normally trade in a day. This is important because the number of potential buyers influences both price and trading ability. Low volume stocks are also referred to as having low or lack of liquidity, or as being thinly traded.

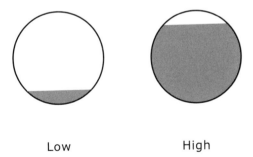

Low                          High

Make sure the average daily trading volume is at least 100 times the number of shares you plan on buying. This way, when you want to sell, you will be fairly likely to have a market for your shares.

*"I guess I'll be much more valuable after this trip."*

# 13

# TRENDS

Trends, like horses. are easier to ride
in the direction they are already going.

*- John Naisbitt*

Back in the late 1800s, Charles Dow studied the behavior of the stock market[6]. He noted that, in any given time frame, the advance or decline of a stock price might form a trend.  Then he discovered that once a trend was formed, it was more likely to continue than reverse.

With this observation, Dow expressed something very simple about how the market behaves.  That observation has proved true every single year since the day he wrote about it.  It is based on a simple observation of the natural process of growth and decline.

If we apply this logic to the precise moment in time when we purchase a stock, the odds change from an even 50/50 chance, to a slight advantage in our favor.  Dow did not, and we cannot mathematically define exactly how great that advantage is.

This doesn't mean that if we buy with a trend we will profit every time, any more than a pair of dice will roll a seven every time, even though it is the most likely combination.

## CLASSIC TREND

The classic way of determining a positive trend is to require a stock price obtain new higher highs and new higher lows over a period of time. Likewise, a negative trend is price movement that creates new lower highs and lower lows in a given time period.

Today there are two ways of understanding trends: graphs, and moving averages.

## GRAPHS

Graphs do provide detailed visual information about price changes. The problem with understanding trends by reading graphs is that they are subject to interpretation and require expertise to read correctly.

However, in order to stay on the positive side of probability concerning trends, we only have to answer one question: Tread or no tread? Therefore, I like to use moving averages instead of graphs since they cut right to the point.

## MOVING AVERAGES

A moving average is the average price of a stock for the past number of days indicated. For example, the 20 day moving average is the average closing price of a stock over the past 20 trading days.

Keep in mind that we are talking trading days, rather than calendar days. A trading day is a day when the stock market is open for business (which is currently five days week or less when a holiday occurs). Therefore, 200 trading days translates into more than 10 months of time; while 20 trading days equals about a month.

Moving averages define price movement and direction with mathematical precision. Therefore it's easy to spot a trend with a moving average; no interpretation is required.

SeeStokRun.com reduces the process to a glance at three moving average indicators; 20, 50 and 200 day (short, medium and long term). It is important to note that the long term trend is considered to be the most influential, or the "underlaying trend," making the shorter ones sub-sets of, or weaker than, the longest one.

## SCALES OF COMPARISON

Charts are usually scaled to the price and performance of the stock they represent. This fact can create enormously misleading perceptions.

For example, if we look at a chart of a stock that went from 2 to 4 in a month, it might look very much like the chart of a stock that went from 80 to 88 in a month.

### PRICE SCALE GRAPHS

Stock A

Price moves from
2 to 4

Stock B

Price moves from
80 to 88

In each case, the top of the graph is determined by the high number and the bottom line of the graph by the low number, regardless of what those numbers represent in terms of value. The charts may look the same, but they represent very different results.

If we look at gains from a standardized perspective, the actual results suddenly appear obvious. They are dramatically different from the picture we got from the price graphs. This understanding is essential in order to make logical decisions.

In this example, the first stock gained 100% (going from 2 to 4), while the second gained

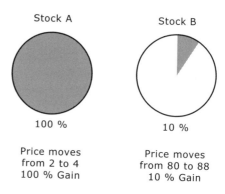

PERCENT SCALE COMPARISON

Stock A

100 %

Price moves
from 2 to 4
100 % Gain

Stock B

10 %

Price moves
from 80 to 88
10 % Gain

only 10% (going from 80 to 88). For this reason SeeStokRun.com translates moving averages and price changes into simple indicators that are calibrated to the same universal scales.

## THE AVERAGE TREND

If we look at all three moving averages side by side, we develop a clear picture of what's going on in different units of time, and therefore whether or not a consistent trend is in progress.

Given that each of the three moving average indicators could be positive, flat or negative, there are a total of 27 combinations possible. Only one of those shows the existence of a positive trend in all three time frames, and is therefore the strongest trend influence.

# 14

# Times

It was the best of times.
It was the worst of times.

*- Charles Dickens*

## Market Climate

Think of the market climate like the weather in terms of its influence on a particular stock you might buy. If it's raining, you might be able to pick the one that will stay dry, but the odds are much better if you start on a sunny day. If the whole market is going down, maybe it's a good time for gardening, golf, or reading a good book, rather than jumping into the market equivalent of a cold thunder storm.

## Top of the Market

Since we know that the market fluctuates, is it smart to buy a stock when it is at its one year high? The assumption many make is that there is a relationship between a stock reaching a new high and the probability that it will go higher. However this is not a determinate piece of information.

I remember during the 1980s and 1990s how people would point to a fast growing stock and say, "It's too expensive," or "It's at the top right now, wait for a correction."

The interesting thing is that many of those stocks just kept climbing year after year with only very minor corrections. The point is, you can't know how much longer a stock will hold a trend. You also can't know if it will keep setting new highs without giving you the chance to pick it up at a lower price.

## MARKET TIMING

Classically "you can't time the market" means that no one can predict the precise moment in time the market will change direction. A more broad definition would be that it's not smart to attempt to benefit from getting in and out of the market at different times.

What is omitted from this train of thought is this: Just because we cannot predict the precise moment the market will change direction, does not mean we cannot observe and react to our advantage when it does. Prediction is not required! Major declines and recoveries don't take place in a flash, they take months and years; plenty of time to react to, and benefit from what **is** happening without needing to predict any precise moment in time.

## DEALING WITH BUBBLES AND CRASHES

Bubbles are normal expressions of extremely positive expectations. Crashes are normal expressions of repressed fears and negative expectations. Both bubbles and crashes will continue to happen from time to time. It is not useful to complain about them or even hope to avoid them. It is much better to accept them as a normal part of the process, and learn to deal with them effectively.

Once you buy a stock the position will either go up or down, and if you're ready for either direction it's like playing an enjoyable game, or watching an interesting experiment.

On the other hand, if you feel uncomfortable, you may want to ask yourself why. Are you prepared? Are you exceeding your risk level?

## PAPER PROFITS

When it comes to selling, keep in mind you haven't actually made any money until you sell. A common mistake people make is they count their profits before they have them. Sure, your account statement might list a neat dollar profit, but always remember, those are not dollars until they are dollars, they are just estimates. Before you sell a stock, what you have are shares of stock, not dollars.

The dollar value estimates of stocks are only valid when the market is actually open and everything is trading normally. That can change at any time, and it can certainly change overnight. This is an inherent risk of the market. The stock market is not a savings account. It is a constantly fluctuating bustling marketplace filled with emotion, greed and sometimes panic.

*"Whoa! Damn it, whoa!"*

# 15

# Stops

> Those who tell you
> it's tough at the top
> have never been to the bottom.
>
> *- Joe Harvey*

Failing to exercise control after purchase is like jumping without a parachute; placing your life in the hands of fate. If your money disappears in one stock, you will lose financial power to invest in another potentially valuable stock.

Stops are one way to apply control. They are pretty easy to understand, even if they do have the ring of jargon.

## Stop Orders

One way to use stops is to place a stop order. Stop orders are public. Once you place a stop order with a brokerage firm, it appears on trading systems all over the world and everyone knows the price at which your shares can be bought or sold.

## Being Taken Out

Since the trigger of a stop order is the market price, once a stop order is placed, both the stop and the trigger are known. What determines the market price is simply the last executed trade price, which in turn can be manipulated by the very next trade. Because of this, stop orders are like published targets that can be "taken out," or "picked off" by big investors, especially when stop orders are placed near the market price.

## PRIVATE STOPS

You may find it smart to keep your stop values to yourself. If you don't tell your broker or enter a stop as a stop order, it will remain private. A private stop is private, and is not a stop order. This means when it's reached, you must then place an order to sell at that time. In the See Stok Run program all portfolio information is kept private, including any alert values you might set.

# 16

# Stop Loss

The first law of holes:
when you're in a hole
you have to stop digging.

*- Benjamin Franklin*

A **stop loss** gets its name from the fact that it does just that, stops your losses. Therefore, a true stop loss is always a point which is below your cost. Since a stop loss is relative to the price you paid for a stock, it is an expression of your personal position and risk toleration.

### Setting a Stop Loss

To set a stop loss alert, figure out how much risk you are willing to take with a particular stock, and make note of a low alert price that is equal to your cost less the percent you are willing risk. Then, if the stock should fall far enough to trigger your alert price, that is your signal to accept a loss on that stock and sell your shares.

Such a strategy produces a sliding scale of results. If you set a stop that is too tight, it will cause you to exit during normal price fluctuations. On the other hand, the more you are willing to let the price decline before selling, the more you will lose if the price keeps going down.

You could set a different stop loss for each stock you own, depending on the behavior or volatility of each stock. Or you could decide on a level of risk that you are comfortable with, and then find stocks that fit within that scope.

Suppose you don't want to risk more than 7% on any one stock. If you find a stock with a flux range greater than 7%, buying such stock under normal conditions could lead you to lose more than you would like to, even within one day. You may even want to find stocks that have fluctuation ranges which are half of your planned risk toleration; this would allow you at least two down market days in a row before hitting your stop loss.

### PERFECT NUMBER

I wish there was a perfect number I could suggest you tolerate before selling, but each stock is different, so there is no magic solution. Also, each person has a different risk tolerance, so you will have to answer these questions according to your own sensibilities.

When you set a stop, you might want to think about the mathematics of decline. A 33% decline requires a 50% gain just to get back to where you started (See chapter 7).

### MIND THE GAP

Stocks can gap right past carefully set stops overnight. If this happens, don't be alarmed. It's all part of the process. If a gap causes you to lose more money than your stop loss anticipated, just accept that unusual event, take the loss, and move on.

### WORSE CASE STOP LOSS SCENARIO

People often ask me, "What's the worse case scenario if I use a stop loss strategy?" Ok, let's play this out.

Let's say you want to take 20 chances to profit in the market and risk 7%. You start by purchasing 10 stocks. Then, in a streak of bad luck, every one of them goes down so far it hits its stop loss and is sold.   At this point about 7% of the capital has been lost.

Then, 10 new stocks are selected and the 93% of remaining capital is reinvested. If each of those stocks also go straight down and hit their stop loss prices, and the positions are sold, at that point about 15% of the original money would have been lost, and about 85% of the capital would remain.

Having said that, I must also warn you that even with stop loss precautions in place, it is possible to lose more than you plan to in a perfect storm.   The market is always risky, and Murphy's law[7] will come into play sooner or later.

If you stick to the rule of never investing more than 50% of your net worth in the market, the most you can lose in stocks is half of your worth.   For advice on how to lose the other half, please read a different book.

## IPO

What about IPOs (Initial Public Offerings)?   If you want to buy a stock which has just hit the market, it will not yet have performance trends or fluctuation ranges.

New stocks tend to bounce around the first few weeks before establishing more stable values.   They are the most unpredictable stocks of all and therefore can represent great opportunities to gain or lose.   But if you want excitement, this could be for you.

# 17

# TRAILING STOPS

A period of continuous bad luck
is as improbable as always staying
on the straight path of virtue.
In both cases,
there will eventually be a cure.

*- Charlie Chaplin*

Once a stock price rises well above your cost, you may want to make
the switch from a stop loss to a trailing stop.

A trailing stop gets its name from the
fact that it trails the price movement
in one direction. Think of it like
pushing a car up hill, and then placing a block (a stop) behind the tires
every now and then so that the car
won't roll back down the hill when
you quit pushing.

A trailing stop is expressed as a percentage less than the highest price
reached by a particular stock while you've been holding it. When a
price falls, the trailing stop remains where it was. It trails the price up,
but stays firmly in place when the price declines in order to stop a free
fall.

For example, a 15% trailing stop, would be equal to the highest market
price held less 15%. When you hear a news story about program trad-

ing in a falling market, much of this trading is being generated by trailing stop programs.

Your objective should be to stay invested in growing stocks for as long as possible, and get out only if they drop significantly. The trailing stop numbers you pick will define what you think is an acceptable fluctuation, and what constitutes a real decline.

## LOSS VS. PROFIT

A stop loss protects capital. A trailing stop protects profit. Therefore, I usually tolerate a slightly greater percentage decline as a trailing stop than I do with a stop loss in an effort to remain invested in potentially growing stocks. This helps save me the trouble of having to sell profitable positions only to reinvest in something else during normal market corrections.

# 18

# RESULTS

> There are risks and costs to
> a program of action but they are
> less than the long-range risks
> and costs of comfortable inaction.
> *- John F. Kennedy*

## PROBABILITY METHOD

What if we apply the probability idea to the three big crashes? This would mean we only buy with a positive trend in place, trailing stop exit, and then buy back in once the 20/50/200 day moving averages are positive again. This is a hypothetical exercise, and I'm not big on those, since life is not lived hypothetically or in the past tense. But since so many people ask about this, here goes just for kicks.

Comparisons will be made using the Dow Jones Industrial Average, and accounting for no other monetary changes[8]. This means I will not discount the value of money for inflation and I will not count any interest that holding cash would normally earn. If these factors were taken into account, the results would be better than illustrated; in the case of the 1929 crash, much better.

Since, on average, it takes 101 days of equal advancement for a 200 day moving average to change from negative to positive, the longest one should have to wait for a 200 day moving average to reverse direction is 101 days. This will be the first point in time at which all three (20, 50 and 200 day) moving averages would be positive after a crash. Therefore we will use 101 days after the market bottom as our buy back point in these examples, even though that point may occur slightly earlier or later.

## 1929

| | | |
|---|---|---|
| Sept 3, 1929 | Market reached its high | 381.17 |
| July 8, 1932 | Market hit bottom | 41.22 |
| Nov 23, 1954 | Market recovered | 382.74 |

After 25 years and 3 months a person who bought and held would finally be back to even money, or about zero profit.

**1929 with a 10% trailing stop:**

| | | |
|---|---|---|
| Sept 30, 1929 | Sell 1.00 share @ | 343.45 |
| Oct 17, 1932 | Buy 5.17 shares @ | 62.69 |

27 days after the high the stop is triggered and the position is sold. Three years later the same capital is reinvested to acquire more shares than were sold. Upon market recovery there is a profit of 417% more than staying in the market would have produced.

## 1987

| | | |
|---|---|---|
| Aug 25, 1987 | Market high | 2,722.42 |
| Oct 19, 1987 | Market bottom | 1,738.74 |
| Aug 24, 1989 | Market recovered | 2,734.64 |

Market recovered in two years; even money.

**1987 with a 10% trailing stop:**

| | | |
|---|---|---|
| Oct 14, 1987 | Sell one share @ | 2,417.70 |
| Mar 14, 1988 | Buy 1.18 shares @ | 2,050.07 |

49 days after the market high we are out of the market. Five months later we buy back in, investing the same capital to acquire more shares than

were sold. On the day of market recovery our 1.18 shares are worth 18% more than remaining invested, and we have a continuing 18% advantage as the market climbs.

## 2000

| Jan 14, 2000 | Market high | 11,722.98 |
| Oct 9, 2002 | Market bottom | 7,286.27 |
| Oct 3, 2006 | Market recovered | 11,727.34 |

Market recovers in over six years; even money.

### 2000 with a 10% trailing stop:

| Feb 11. 2000 | Sell one share @ | 10,425.21 |
| Mar 6, 2003 | Buy 1.36 shares @ | 7,673.99 |

27 days after the market high we are out of the market. More than three years later we buy back in, investing the same capital to acquire more shares than were sold. On recovery our 1.36 shares were worth at least 36% more than staying invested, with a continuing 36% advantage as the market climbs.

Of course if you pick different trailing stop percentages, you will get different results. Here's a list of some other results.

| Stop date: | Percent stop: | On Recovery: |
| --- | --- | --- |
| *1929 Crash* | | |
| Oct 3, 1929 | 12% stop | +428% |
| Oct 19, 1929 | 15% stop | +419% |
| | | |
| *1987 Crash* | | |
| Oct 15, 1987 | 12% stop | +15% |
| Oct 16, 1987 | 15% stop | +10% |

| Stop date: | Percent stop: | On Recovery: |
|---|---|---|
| *2000 Crash* | | |
| Feb 18, 2000 | 12%  stop | +33% |
| Feb 25, 2000 | 15%  stop | +29% |

## NO PROOF

The stock market is a part of the real world, where things beyond our imagination can and do happen each and every year. Sure I can create a spiffy little model that will produce fantastic results with historical data. So what? The past is not only a sitting duck, it is a very well known sitting duck. The real test is in the present and your ability to control what is happening today while facing the blank unknown future. There is no proof of the future.

# 19

# MULTIPLE EXITS

Perhaps there is only one
cardinal sin: impatience.

*- Franz Kafka*

It's common to think that selling a position is an all or nothing proposition. People ask only, "Should I sell, or not?" In reality there are a range of options.

If you are lucky enough to hold a stock with a substantial gain, you may want to consider only selling a portion of your shares if and when the price drops to hit your trailing stop, and then create another trailing stop at that point in time.

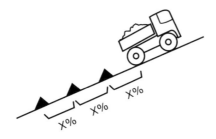

In this way you will be likely to capture some profits if your holding suffers a temporary decline, while at the same time staying partially invested, with the chance of profiting if the position recovers and continues growing. This method saves you at least half the agony of the first trailing stop selling point decision. You will be taking some profit, while continuing to hold on to remaining profit potential.

The greater your profits, and the larger number of shares you have, the more exit points you may wish to add.

# 20

# PROFIT TAKING

> Haste in every business
> brings failure.
>
> *- Herodotus*

If you talk to most any non-professional investor that has made life changing profits in the market, chances are fairly good they did so by profiting greatly from just one stock that kept sky-rocketing for years. If you hold on to a strongly growing stock this will keep increasing your percentage risk in that one stock as time goes by. This could pay off big, or you could end up giving significant gains back to the market if that one stock drops quickly.

> SINCE THE MARKET IS AND WILL REMAIN
> EVER UNPREDICTABLE,
> IT CAN BE SMART TO BANK A FEW DOLLARS,
> EVEN WHEN THINGS LOOK LIKE THEY'RE
> GETTING BETTER ALL THE TIME.

One way to protect yourself while continuing to profit is to sell just a small bit of a large stock gain, perhaps 5% or 10% of that stock. This is like taking a small slice of cake. The interesting thing is, if a stock keeps growing, you can keep doing this repeatedly while continuing to hold shares.

*"What burns me up is that the answer is right here somewhere, staring us in the face."*

# 21

# ENTRANCE STYLES

> You can't get what you want,
> 'till you know what you want.
>
> *- Joe Jackson*

## WAYS TO PICK

People go about picking stocks all sorts of ways. Beside the fundamental and technical approaches, people follow formal or casual advice, hunches, or sift through stocks by criteria to find ones that fit their idea of what will lead to good results. Regardless of the possible success of a random selection, few use that method. The interesting thing is that I can find no compelling reason to use only one way, or one logic to select stocks for purchase. In fact, picking portions of your portfolio according to various methods is another illustration of potential diversification. There is no need to select every stock you buy according to the same reasoning.

## STAGING

One way to smooth things out as you enter the market, and therefore help insure that your entry is a calm experience instead of a wild ride, is to exercise some patience. Consider multiple times of entry. I call this a staged entrance. If you enter different stocks at different times you will also be entering slightly different market climates.

Stocks are influenced by the performance of the industrial sectors they are a part of, as well as the performance of the market as a whole. Because of this, if you enter many positions at the same time, they could all be positively, or negatively impacted by a geopolitical event, therefore yielding similar results.  However, if you buy different positions at different times, each will take on a slightly different historical relationship to market influences.

If you happen to pick the perfect moment to enter the market, a staged entrance will produce a somewhat lower result.  On the other hand, if you happen to pick the perfectly wrong moment to enter the market, a staged entrance will save you from losing lots of money.

### My way

Personally, I buy for all sorts of reasons, such as, I like a product, I see a company with an advantage, I spot a trend in society, I see innovation, or I just have a positive feeling, a hunch about a company.  Usually I don't spend much time or thought on it, but instead rely on basic impressions.  The more detailed information I need in order to see the value in a stock, the less likely I'll buy it.  Then I check to see if it has a positive trend, enough volume and a reasonable fluctuation range.

In the case of an IPO, since there is no trend, fluctuation or volume numbers to consult, I skip that, and just dive in if it feels right.

The point is, I start somewhere, almost anywhere, because I'm very clear about the fact I really don't know what any stock is going to do in the future, and I don't pretend.  I'm also very clear that I will sell if it goes down to my stop loss, and hold if it goes up.  When I buy a stock that goes down, it's no big deal because I get out quickly, losing very little money.  This allows me to take controlled risks even though I spend almost no time thinking about what stocks to buy.  That's my haphazard method.  Should you do it this way?  I don't know.

### Your way

What feels right to you?  Do you want to read the Wall Street Journal, investment magazines or Value Line[9] to search for ideas of stocks to buy?

Do you like to use internet sorting tools to find stocks that fit particular criteria, or study graphs? Does throwing darts appeal to you? Do what you like, what seems right to you, what you have the time to accomplish.

You could ignore trends and choose to bank on your assessment of fundamental value, and hold on to positions without any stops in place, but then you should also be willing to accept the results, whatever they might be.

The point is to find a style of both entering and exiting stocks that agrees with your beliefs and your risk comfort level. I can't tell you what this is, but I encourage you to create a plan that fits with your personality and your risk comfort level.

In any case if you use SeeStokRun.com software you will at least be able to blatantly see the performance of your portfolio.

## STARTING

When we first start something new, our expectations are likely to be fully engaged, so it is important to prepare for the ride. No matter what happens, people tend to overreact to their first experiences. If the first couple of trades go well, they are convinced they are brilliant. If the first few trades go poorly, they are convinced the system doesn't work.

If you are in the market long enough, there will be plenty of occasions to experience both moves in your favor and against you. See if you can put your expectations aside and have the cool mindset of a mathematician. Instead of saying to yourself, "I think this one is heading up," say, "I'm going to buy this one and see what happens." This will help you be prepared to take any action required.

Even if you plan a staged entrance, it's a good idea to buy at least three stocks to start. This will give you some diversification right away, and help keep you from focusing on the performance of any one stock.

## TESTING

If you're not sure where to set stops, or you're not used to buying and selling stocks, it is a good idea to do some testing with small money first. To test, buy a very small amount of stock and do a trial run to see how things work. Practice is essential to build confidence and prevent panic. I strongly recommend testing and experimenting with small dollars until you feel comfortable. However, when you invest larger dollars don't expect the results to match your test. The market will do what it will.

# 22

# SEE

> Why, sometimes I've believed as many as
> six impossible things before breakfast.
>
> *- Lewis Carrol*

## WHY SEE STOK?

 So why go to the trouble of creating a data animation software program that makes portfolio management largely a visual process? Why not read a normal brokerage statement, or use a typical web site with a spread sheet of stock positions? The answer is that animated visual imagery can create cognitive short cuts and bring about enlightening revelations which are extremely valuable.

Before we become aware, we must first perceive something and enter into a thought process. The trouble is, both perception and cognition occur so quickly and frequently within the human mind, that most of us take the process for granted. If we look at the cognitive chain of events when applied to reading a document, such as a stock portfolio, it goes something like this:

1. Perception:          We see it!  Black marks on paper.

2. Sense or nonsense:   What's that?  The mind applies symbolic meaning to the marks.  Are they letters? Pictures?  Useless scribbles?

3. Symbol conversion:   What symbols are they?  What language?  Is MMLXXXVIII the same as deux mille quatre-vingt quatre?  Is there meaning?

4. Symbol Context:   Do the symbols link together?  What am I reading about?  What is the theme?

5. Relative Meaning:   What is it to me?  Is 2,088 a lot of money or a little?  How does it relate to my world?

6. Decisional Meaning:  How does this compare to my beliefs?  Is it good, bad, amusing, helpful or alarming?

7. Decision Making:   What do I want to do? Keep reading, stop reading, research, or take action?

## BARRIERS

That's a lot of steps, and usually the mind travels through them so quickly we don't even notice.   However, when difficulty with one or more of these steps presents itself, many, if not most people simply stop.  What did you do when you came to the Roman numeral above?  Did you stop and figure it out, or skip past?  Did you recognize the French language, and know the number, or did you just keep reading without knowing?  Numbers don't lend themselves to easy understanding when their relational complexity builds past just a few elements.

## SOLUTION

What we commonly call intuition is that gigantic bank of knowledge and logic that resides deep within our mind at the sub-conscious level.  The mind is fully capable of understanding extremely complex situations at an intuitive level in a flash, but only when information is presented in a manner that the mind can easily absorb.

Complex numeric relationships are not physical things. We can't see them, and therefore they usually don't engage our higher intuitional abilities. However with the right imagery you can see in a glance the important relational perspectives, thereby skipping much of the normal cognitive process, while providing more enlightening understanding at the same time.

THE PROCESS OF REDUCTION

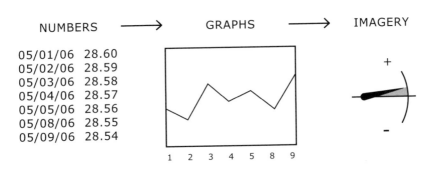

IN TERMS OF INTUITIVE UPTAKE:
GRAPHS ARE BETTER THAN NUMBERS.
RESULTS ORIENTED IMAGES ARE BETTER THAN GRAPHS.

The image at the far right above is an example of information reduction to a clear image which instantly delivers the most important information being sought. Of course this approach only works well if the person creating the image understands the decision making objectives of the viewer and the relative importance of the data.

All material happiness
is based on figures.

*- Honoré de Balzac*

# Overall Review

### Enter well

- Risk according to your understanding and comfort level.
- Learn and test the brokerage system you use.
- Use whatever method you like to pick stocks, or several ways at once.
- Buy at least 3 at first, and aim to hold 10 or more over time.
- Buy a mix of stocks in different industries; diversify.
- Buy with positive trends; 20/50/200 day moving averages.
- Pick a percentage stop loss that you are willing to risk, and then enforce it, emotions aside.
- Do not buy stocks that have daily fluctuations which are more than half your stop loss percentage.
- Require average volumes at least 100 times greater than the number of shares you will hold.
- Spend no more than 10% of your portfolio value buying one stock.

### Monitor well

- Watch your portfolio! It only takes a couple of minutes.
- Compare stocks using standardized scales of measurement.
- Use visual software to gain access to your intuition.

### Exit well

- Stop your losses by plan, and stay within your risk level.
- Hold rising stocks and use trailing stops to capture profits in the event a real decline takes place.
- Take small slices of profit from highly gaining positions every now and then.

*"This is so cool! I'm flying this thing completely on my Palm pilot!"*

# 23

# Bon Voyage !

> Men travel faster now,
> but I do not know if they
> go to better things.
> *- Willa Cather*

I hope you now have enough ideas to create an investment plan that fits with who you are, both your tolerance for risk and your available time.

## Enjoyment

If investing in the stock market is such serious business that you can't possibly enjoy it, then I would guess you are risking too much, or at least too much for your personality. To play this game well, a calm hand and a light heart are great assets.

## Ethical Considerations

On the moral side of life, I see no need to sacrifice ethical concerns in order to be a good investor. Given that there are many opportunities to profit in the market, why needlessly tread on your own ethical standards? Although, in our complicated and compromised world, it is extremely difficult to have complete ethical purity, you can make choices that matter.

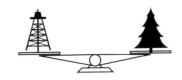

As a rule, I avoid companies whose main line of business is something I think is harmful to our planet or our society. I may not be able to discourage certain businesses, but there is no need to contribute to them by investing. The most effective votes we make in our world today, are those made when we spend and invest. If you do want to have a positive impact on the world, a great place to start is by placing your dollars well.

## RESOURCES

If you are interested in learning more or would like to discover what has happened since this book was published, please check out these resources:

The software:        SeeStokRun.com

The book:            inkVoice.com

## ALOHA!

May you have all the best fortune taking chances in life!

## GLOSSARY

Analyst - A professional who is paid to analyze stocks and the companies which issue the stocks.

Annual Basis - A number adjusted for its annual effect, or a number considered only once a year. So, for example, an invesment that earns 1% per month, would be equal to earning 12% on an annual basis.

Asset Allocation - The process of allocating portions of one's assets among various classes of investment (such as stocks, bonds, cash and real estate), or among various industrial sectors within the stock market. See page 32.

Averaging - The practice of determining the net results of a given group of investments by taking the average of the entire group. See page 29.

Averaging In - The practice of buying the same stock repeatedly over a period of time as its price changes, thereby establishing a cost for all shares which is the average price paid for all shares. This practice treats stocks as if they were a savings account (which they are not).

Bear Market - A period of time during which most stocks are going down in value.

Benchmark - A point of reference by which to judge results. The most common stock market benchmarks are the Dow Jones Industrial Average, and the S&P 500. However, both of these may go negative, making it possible to out perform those benchmarks and still lose money.

Beta - An indicator of a stock's relative volatility compared to the market as a whole as a multiplier, such that a beta of 1 is equal to normal market volatility, a beta of 2 is twice as volatile. See page 36.

Bonds - Legal instruments which place things of value as collateral in exchange for borrowing money from investors. Bonds are usually issued by a corporation or government which pays interest to the holder in exchange for the use of their money.

Broker - Any professional who trades, or processes trades in the stock market for a brokerage house.

Bubble - A period of time during which a stock rises sharply in price, and then declines to a previous more stable level.

Bull Market - A period of time during which most stocks are producing positive price gains.

Buy and Hold - The strategy of buying and indefinitely holding a position in the stock market with no exit plan.

Commodities - Shares of actual physical resources which are traded in the open market, such as grain, fuel and metal. Such shares are based on the type of resource, such as bushels of wheat, barrels of oil, or head of cattle.

Computerized Exchanges - Computer networks established for trading stock. See also: ECN.

Consolidation of a trend - A point in the life of a trend during which the growth or decline of the trend slows almost to a stop, and then later returns on its merry way.

Correction of a trend - A point in the life of a trend during which the growth or decline reverses for a short period of time, and then continues as before.

Cut Loss - Same as "Stop Loss."

Cycles - Periods of time when stocks seem to repeat past tendencies.

Decimal Pricing - The expression of stock prices as decimals instead of the old way which was by the use of fractions. Most stocks are now represented by numbers accurate to the fourth place after the decimal, as in 0.0001, or one one-hundredth of a penny.

Decline - A period of time during which the price of a stock mainly goes down in price.

Depression - A significant period of time during which the stock market, the economy and employment decline. Also; a dip in the road, a low pressure weather system, and a really bad feeling.

Discount Internet Stock Trading - Trading systems that charge much lower rates than formerly offered by typical stock brokers, and now made available through the internet. See also ECN.

Derivatives - Any investment vehicle which derives its value or price from the value of some other investment, such as a stock. There are a host of complex derivatives.

Diversification - The practice of investing among several different classifications of holdings in an attempt to reduce risk. See page 30.

Dow Jones Industrial Average - One of the main market indexes, established by the Dow Jones company, containing 30 stocks of the largest US companies traded on the NYSE.

ECN - Electronic Communications Networks, which are networks setup to trade stocks, frequently outside of the standard market and at times before or after normal trading hours.

Entrance - The process of selecting a stock, a number of shares to buy and buying those shares; this is entering a position.

Exit - The process of selling some or all of a position.

Fluctuations - The normal and nearly constant price movements that stocks experience, both up and down, on a daily basis.

Functional Risk - A person's practical dollar exposure on any given day, taking into account that person's trading knowledge of the market, their ability to trade out of the positions they hold, and their total capital worth. See page 25.

Fundamentalists - Those who believe that the key to predicting the future price of a stock is found in studying information about the company issuing the stock.

Fundamental Information - There is no clear definition as to what is or is not fundamental corporate information.  Normally the stock price, estimated earnings, outstanding shares, accounting practices, business development plans, management experience, past growth record and asset values are consiered fundamental information.

Hedge Funds -  Funds that trade investments in ways that are considered high risk in order to seek higher profits while "hedging" against loss. This frequently includes the practice of short selling.  Such funds are therefore usually limited to investment by those who are wealthy enough to absorb significant loses.

Holding - An investment that one holds. Also known as a "position."

Index - A collection of stocks compiled for the purpose of establishing a performance gage of an investment sector.  See page 23.

Index Investing - The practice of investing in a fund that is designed to mimic the performance of an index.

Insured Bonds -  Bonds which are insured in an effort to guarantee their worth.

Limit Order - An order to buy or sell shares of stock at a stated price or better.

Long - The word long is used two different ways regarding stock investing. "Going long" or "being long" in a stock usually means that one has bought shares of stock in a typical way and hopes they will go up in value; this is the opposite of "going short" or "short selling" a stock.  The other way the word long is used is to express a stock investment that has been held for a year or more, thereby qualifying for capital gains tax rates for long term investments, as opposed to short term (less than a year) investments which are taxed at income tax rates.

Market Climate - Refers to the overall market trend.

Market Makers - A company that owns significant amounts of a stock and normally offers for trade (to buy and sell) shares of that stock at publicly stated prices.

Market Order - An order entered with a brokerage firm to trade (buy or sell) shares of a stock at the market price.

Market Price - The price reported by the market of the last trade made.

Market Timing - The practice of attempting to guess when the market will reverse its current trend and benefit thereby and/or the practice of investing and divesting in the market depending on its general direction. See page 44.

Mathematics of Decline - The difference between the percentage loss of capital, and the percent the remaining capital must gain in order to recover the lost capital. See page 19.

Moving Averages - A moving average is the average of the closing prices for the past number of days indicated. See page 40.

Mutual Fund - An investment fund that is owned mutually by a large group of investors. Typically mutual funds invest in many different holdings or stocks, and often the fund managers charge the fund a fee, or "load" for their management services.

NYSE - The New York Stock Exchange. The oldest and most traditional stock market in the United States, highlighted by big older companies.

NASDAQ - The largest and most modern electronic stock trading market in the United States.

Options - An option is an agreement which gives the holder the right to buy or sell shares at some future time depending on the future price of the stock or commodity.

P/E Ratio - Price over Earnings ratio: A stock's current price divided by its estimated earnings per share for the next year. For example, if a stock's price was 10 dollars a share, and the company estimated it would earn 1 dollar for every outstanding share of stock in the market, its P/E ratio would be 10. To state it differently, a P/E of 10 means that 10 years worth of a company's earnings would equal its stock price. Generally speaking, the higher a company's P/E ratio, the higher are the market expectations of its success, realistic or not.

Perceived Risk - A person's perception of how predictable the future prospects of any investment are; the more unpredictable, the higher the risk.   See page 25.

Position - An investment that one owns. Also known as a "holding."

Private Stop - A stop, or predetermined selling price, which one keeps privately, with the plan of entering a market order to sell if and when that stop is reached. See page 48.

Program Trading -   The practice of allowing a computer to execute actual trades automatically upon reaching specified criteria.

Recession -   A significantly long period of time during which the economy is slowly declining and generally lackluster.

Recovery - The point in time when a stock price reaches the same level it was prior to a decline.

Reversal -   When a trend changes direction and goes the other way.

Reverse Split -   When a company recalls its shares and issues fewer shares for each previously existing share.  For example, a 1 for 2 split (noted 1:2) would be called a reverse split, since for every two shares previously held, stockholders would receive one share of the new issue.  On the day a reverse split takes effect in the market, the price will be corrected accordingly to result in the same dollar value.  For example, if the price was 10 dollars per share before the split (or 2 shares = $20), on the day of the split the price would be adjusted to 20 dollars (or 1 share = $20).

Risk - The possibility of loss.

Risk Management -   The practice of following a logical plan with the goal of reducing one's functional risk levels.

See Stok Run Program - The software service produced by Animated Equity, LLC. This service provides stock performance information and allows visual portfolio monitoring. It is available on the web at: seestokrun.com.

Short Selling - The practice of borrowing someone else's shares of stock and selling them with the hope of buying them back at a lower price in order to return the borrowed shares and profit by the difference. Since, after shares are sold short, the short seller is responsible for replacing those shares in the future, no matter what price they achieve, there is no theoretical limit to the amount of money that can be lost if the share price rises instead of falls. Therefore this practice is extremely high risk.

S&P 500 - An index of 500 large company stocks created by the Standard & Poors company.

Split - When a company issues additional shares of stock to every previously existing stockholder. For example, a 2 for 1 split (noted 2:1) would result in the company issuing an additional share for every share previously held. On the day the split takes effect in the market, the price will be corrected accordingly to result in the same dollar value. For example, if the price was 10 dollars per share before the split (or 1 share = $10), on the day of the split the price would be adjusted to 5 dollars (or 2 shares = $10).

Staged entrance - The process of investing in the market by buying positions in various stocks over a period of several weeks or months. See page 63.

Stock Market - The generic name for many of the different markets that exist for the purpose of trading stocks.

Stop Limit - A stop order consisting of two price values, a stop price and a limit price, which becomes an active order to sell at the limit price or better when the stop price is reached.

Stop Loss - A stop price, which is below cost and is designed for the purpose of stopping one from experiencing further losses.

Stop Market - A stop order to sell shares at the market price when the stop price is reached.

Stop Order - Official instructions, or orders, placed with a brokerage to trade shares of stock if and when the price reaches the stop value. See page 47.

Stop Trigger -   The stop price that triggers an action, such as selling.

Trailing Stop - A stop which is set and reset by calculating a certain percentage less than the highest price reached since a position has been held, thereby trailing the price in one direction only.

Technical Theories - Stock investing theories based on the idea that one can determine the future price movement of a stock based on patterns formed by past movements.

Trend - A recognizable pattern of growth or decline (during the time frame considered) wherein new higher highs and higher lows in an positive trend, or new lower lows and new lower highs in a negative trend, are set. The examples below illustrate the three most basic trend changes in a positive trend.

POSSIBLE TREND CHANGES

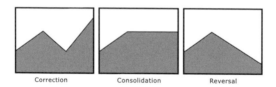

Correction          Consolidation          Reversal

## ENDNOTES

1. *Take On The Street,* Arthur Levitt (former SEC Chairman), Pantheon Books, 2002. An excellent book regarding the inside workings of the stock market and corporate America. See especially Chapter 5, The Numbers Game.

2. A cinnamon-ring tail cebus monkey from Brazil named Mr. Monk picks stocks, and does pretty well. For more information, see the Chicago Sun-Times' Monkey Manager stock picking contest.

3. From 1971 to 1980, 74% of pension funds performed below the S&P 500 average; which means only 26% of professionally managed funds did better than the average of 500 non-managed stocks. *Bogle on Mutual Funds: New Perspective for the Intelligent Investor,* John C. Bogle, (New York: Irwin Professional Publishing) 1994.
   "Our results indicate that there are significant advantages to indexing. When examining a single index as compared with each fund category, and setting aside the small company equity funds, we find the indices significantly outperform the mutual funds in 25 out of 30 possible cases." *Indexing vs. Active Management,* by Rich Fortin, Ph.D. and Stuart Michelson, Ph.D.
   See also: *Active vs. Passive Management for Small-Cap Funds,* by Jim Wiandt, March 19, 2001 *What Risk Premium Is "Normal"?* by Robert D. Arnott and Peter L. Bernstein, Financial Analysts Journal, March/April 2002, Vol. 58, No. 2.

4. The Dow Jones Industrial Average is an index created by Dow Jones and Company, Inc. of 30 of the largest companies. Other Dow Jones indexes exist. This company also publishes the Wall Street Journal.

5. The S&P 500 is an index created by Standard and Poors of 500 of the largest companies.

6. Charles Dow lived, Nov. 6, 1851–Dec. 4, 1902. An extraordinary journalist who co-founded Dow Jones & Company and The Wall Street Journal. He invented the Dow Jones Industrial Average and defined principles for understanding and analyzing stock market behavior. He did not complete high school. See: *Charles H. Dow: economist;* a selection of his writings on business cycles. Edited, with comments, by George W. Bishop, Jr., by Dow, Charles Henry, 1851-1902. Princeton, N.J., Dow Jones Books [c1967]

7. Murphy's law states: "If anything can go wrong, it will." It was coined at Edwards Air Force Base in 1949 and named after Capt. Edward A. Murphy, an engineer working on Air Force Project MX981, which was designed to see how much sudden deceleration a person can stand in a crash. As the lives of the test subjects were in his hands, Murphy did his best to account for every possible potential point of failure.

8. Crash data for 1929 and 1987 from: Dow Jones Averages 1885-1990, Edited by Phyllis S. Pierce, Homewood Illinois, Business One Irwin.

9. Value Line is a publication of Value Line Publishing Inc. It is a service that provides detailed information on companies and their stocks.

## ABOUT THE AUTHOR

Gray Purdy is a life long private investor, the founder of Animated Equity, LLC (a data animation software company), and the designer of SeeStokRun.com, a stock market monitoring program. To enable his visual ideas, he invented the patented software known as a Method, Apparatus and Computer-readable Medium for Altering the Appearance of an Animated Object. An avid artist, he paints oil on canvas in the impressionistic style, and strives to promote actions which help care for the delicate planet we call earth.

To order copies of this book online,
please visit: inkVoice.com